BIRDS

FROM FOREST TO
FAMILY ROOM

BIRDS

FROM FOREST TO
FAMILY ROOM

John
Zeaman

Before They Were Pets

FRANKLIN WATTS
New York London Hong Kong Sydney
Danbury, Connecticut

Cover and interior design by Robin Hoffmann/Brand X Studios
Illustrations by Steve Savage

Photographs ©: Photographs ©: AKG London: 42 (Paris, Bibliotheque Nationale), 17, 26; Animals Animals: 51 (Arthur Gloor); Art Resource: 50 (Fine Art Photographic Library, London), 29 (Erich Lessing); BBC Natural History Unit: 35 (Gerry Ellis), 25 (Jeff Foott), 40 (Nick Garbutt), 14 (Brian Lightfoot), 8 (Dietmar Nill), cover, bottom right (Warwick Sloss), 34 (Mark & Juliet Yates); Corbis-Bettmann: 11, 33; E.T. Archive: 20; ENP Images: 10 (Walt Enders), 6 (Steve Gettle); Photo Researchers: cover, center (Alan L. Detrick), 21, 36 bottom (Kenneth W. Fink), 24 (David Hosking), 45 (M.P. Kahl), cover, top right, 38 (J.M. Labat), 15, 28 (Tom McHugh), 49 (Hans Reinhard), 2 (H. Reinhard/Okapia); Superstock, Inc. 31 (Bibliotheque Nationale, Paris/ Bridgeman Art Library), 9; Tony Stone Images: 39, cover, top left (Tim Davis), 12 (Frans Lanting), 16 (Renee Lynn), 22 (Martin Rogers), 44 (Jean-Marc Truchet); UPI/Corbis-Bettmann: 53; Visuals Unlimited: 18 (Kjell B. Sandved); Wildlife Collection: 36 top right, 36 top left (Martin Harvey), cover, bottom left (Tom Vezo), 47 (Steffan Widstrand).

Visit Franklin Watts on the Internet at:
http://publishing.grolier.com

Library of Congress Cataloging-in-Publication Data
Zeaman, John.
Birds: from forest to family room / John Zeaman.
p. cm. — (Before they were pets)
Includes bibliographical references and index.
Summary: Discusses the history and process of domesticating a variety of birds, including geese, chickens, pigeons, raptors, parrots, and canaries.
ISBN 0-531-20351-4 (lib.bdg.)   0-531-15948-5 (pbk.)
1. Cage birds—Juvenile literature.   2. Birds—Juvenile literature.
3. Beneficial birds— Juvenile literature. [1. Birds. 2. Domestic animals.] I. Title. II. Series: Zeaman, John. Before they were pets.
SF461.35.Z43   1999
636.5—dc21   98-2706
                                                                    CIP
                                                                     AC

GROLIER
PUBLISHING

CONTENTS

The bright colors and beautiful song of the goldfinch make it easy to spot.

INTRODUCTION

Throughout history, people have admired birds more than any other creatures on Earth. These feathered animals enchant us with their melodious songs and brilliant colors. Using their highly developed **syrinx**—or voice box—some birds can imitate our speech and a variety of other sounds. Birds may have even inspired early humans to learn to sing. Birds also have highly developed eyes. Like us, they see all the world's vivid colors. They use color to locate sources of food, such as nectar, and to attract mates.

What fascinates us most about birds, though, is their ability to fly. Have you ever seen a hawk soar high above the ground and suddenly swoop down to snatch up

Voice Box

How are birds able to talk and sing? A bird, like a person, has a voice box. Their voice box, called a syrinx, is set in the lower part of the windpipe. When air passes through it, ribbonlike membranes vibrate, creating croaks, trills, and even words.

An owl in flight

prey? Have you watched a flock of geese fly in a v-shaped formation? Has an owl flown past you on its ghostly night passage? We are captivated by what birds can do—and so were our ancestors.

People who lived 10,000 years ago painted birds on the walls of the caves they lived in. They also etched images of birds—owls, cranes, eagles, and ravens—on ancient bone tools. Many of the gods and goddesses worshiped by people living in the world's earliest civilizations had bird-shaped heads or were able to fly.

For many centuries, humans could only dream of flying like the birds. It was not until 1903 that this dream became a reality. Today, we fly in airplanes with wings shaped like those of a bird.

Thoth, the ancient Egyptian god of wisdom and writing, had the head of a bird and the body of a person.

BIRDS IN HISTORY

Humans and birds have had a close relationship for thousands of years. Birds have hunted with us, carried messages, participated in races, entertained us with their songs, and served as a source of food. They were probably

HOW DO BIRDS FLY?

A bird's wing is streamlined to cut through the air easily. When a bird lifts its wings during flight, some of the feathers spread apart to let air through. This makes it easier for the bird to raise its wings. As the bird lowers its wings, the feathers overlap to press firmly against the air.

Birds can also glide, without flapping their wings, for short periods. Some birds, such as the hawks and eagles, can soar. Rising air currents propel them upward.

A great egret in flight

the first animals **tamed** simply for their beauty. In fact, humans may have kept birds in cages made of twigs before they developed written language.

The ancient Sumerians, who lived about 8,000 years ago in an area that is now part of the Middle East, used the word "subura" to describe a birdcage. In ancient

This 400-year-old painting shows a wealthy Muslim gentleman with his falcon.

Clever Crows

Crows, also called ravens, often work together to get food. Several may land on the ground next to a feeding animal. While they distract the animal, another crow swoops down and snatches the food away. Then, they all fly off and share the feast.

In ancient Rome, many wealthy people kept exotic birds such as these scarlet macaws.

India, myna birds and parakeets were displayed in festive parades. About 2,400 years ago, a Greek man named Glaucon raised and sold quails, cranes, peacocks, and many different types of songbirds as pets. Birds were also popular pets in the ancient Aztec city of Tenochtitlan, which is now part of Mexico.

About 2,300 years ago, Roman soldiers conquered parts of India and brought home spices, cotton clothes, and parrots. Many wealthy Romans bought the parrots; some even had slaves to train and care for the birds. Some Romans also kept pet ravens and taught them to talk.

1

BRINGING BIRDS INTO OUR LIVES

EVOLUTION OF BIRDS

Birds have lived on Earth far longer than humans have. In fact, birds were here when the dinosaurs ruled the world. Some ancient birds lived in the fields and forests. Others could be found in wetlands or along the shores of lakes and oceans. While some of these early **species** of birds are now **extinct**, many are still around today.

You may be surprised to hear that many scientists think that birds are descended from a group of small dinosaurs called the coelurosaurs. These dinosaurs ran standing up on their hind legs and balanced with their tails, just as birds do today.

Scaly Feet

Birds do not look much like the reptiles they evolved from—until you look at their feet. The scales and sharp nails of birds are very similar to those of lizards.

Dinosaurs, including coelurosaurs, were **cold-blooded**—their body temperature changed as the air temperature of their environment changed. When the air temperature was cold, the dinosaur's breathing and heartbeat slowed down. As a result, they could not move very quickly. Most modern descendants of the dinosaurs are cold-blooded, too. Have you ever seen a snake lying on a dark rock on a sunny morning? It was warming up so it could move fast enough to catch its breakfast.

Warm-blooded animals, such as humans and other **mammals**, can regulate their body temperature. As long

An adder warming itself in the morning sun.

This display at a zoo includes models of some of the earliest birds.

as you are healthy, your body temperature stays at about 98.6°F (37°C). And because your body temperature does not change with the air temperature, you can stay active all the time.

No one is sure how the cold-blooded coelurosaurs developed into warm-blooded birds. Some scientists think a few coelurosaurs had loose, overlapping scales that protected, or insulated, them from extreme temperatures. Over time, these scales **evolved** into feathers, which are excellent insulators, and eventually these animals learned to regulate their body temperature internally. As a result, they could use their feathers for other purposes. Some used their feathers to help them move around. Eventually,

15

FEATHERS

Birds are the only living things with feathers. Each feather has three main parts:

- the shaft (or quill), which is hollow at the thick end;
- the barbs, which grow from both sides of the shaft;
- the barbules, tiny fringes that grow from the barbs.

Over time, a bird's feathers wear out and must be replaced. Some birds **molt**—lose their feathers and grow new ones—three times a year. Most birds lose only a few feathers at a time, so that they can always fly to find food or escape from enemies. But water birds, such as ducks and geese, often lose all their flight feathers at once. Before they molt, these birds fly to a large body of water where they are relatively safe and can find plenty of food. Migrating birds always molt in the late summer or early fall, so they will have strong new feathers for their long flight.

Do you see the shaft, barbs, and barbules of these feathers?

these creatures developed wings and tails, which allowed them to fly.

The oldest bird **fossil** ever discovered is about 140 million years old. The pigeon-sized skeleton has a jaw with teeth rather than a beak, claws on its fingers, and a long bony tail. At first, it seems more similar to a modern lizard than a modern bird.

Scientists classify it as the earliest known ancestor of birds because it has one feature that modern **reptiles** lack—feathers. The rock that the skeleton was found in has imprints of feathers along the forelimbs and down the tail. Nobody knows how well this animal, called Archaeopteryx, could fly—or if it could fly at all. It may have only been able to glide from tree to tree. It is also possible that Archaeopteryx used its feathers as a net for catching small insects.

How Many Feathers Does a Bird Have?

The bigger the bird, the more feathers it has. A farmer once counted 8,325 feathers on a female chicken. A swan has about 25,200 feathers. Some small songbirds may have as few as 1,100 feathers.

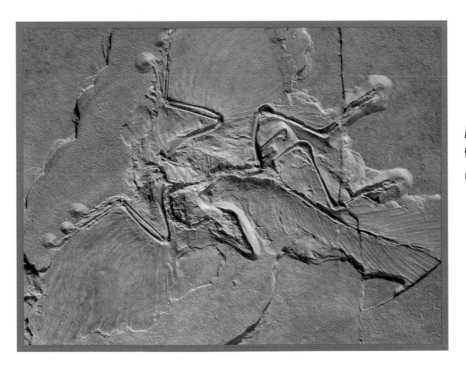

A fossil of Archaeopteryx, the oldest known ancestor of birds

17

There are very few other fossils of early birds. Because birds are small and their bones are lightweight, their remains are not often found as fossils. Nevertheless, scientists have been able to piece together enough information to know that the first true birds lived about 100 million years ago. By 60 million years ago, many modern families of birds had evolved.

Today, birds are one of the most successful groups of animals. There are about 9,700 different species. Birds

Penguins have no problem surviving in the bitter cold climate of Antarctica.

are found on every continent and in nearly every ecosystem on Earth. Every species of modern bird owes its success to the long-extinct reptile that grew feathers.

OUR FIRST ENCOUNTERS WITH BIRDS

Our first interest in birds was probably as a source of food. Soon after people began to settle down and live in villages, they started to keep birds in cages for extended periods of time. People realized that if they raised a single bird, its eggs could provide many meals. These ancient people probably also used bird feathers to make clothing and decorations.

Soon they discovered that some birds are easier to keep than others. Over time, these birds were **bred** to develop birds that are more gentle and more meaty than their wild ancestors. Breeding has more far-reaching effects than taming. Taming involves teaching one animal to act in a certain way. Breeding involves raising successive generations of animals in order to bring out qualities, or **traits**, that make that species more useful to humans or easier to live with. These qualities are passed from parent to child by **genes** located in an animal's cells. Each gene has information that determines what an animal looks like and, to some extent, how it behaves.

When an animal has inherited certain characteristics that make it better suited to live with humans from its parents and grandparents, it is said to be **domesticated**. In other words, just because a bird is kept captive doesn't mean that it's domesticated. Some kinds of birds are very difficult to domesticate. The ancient Egyptians were unable to tame or domesticate the Egyptian goose, which they considered sacred. They also had difficulty domesticating

Hollow Bones

In order to fly, a bird must be lightweight. As birds evolved from reptiles, they developed hollow bones that look a lot like dry macaroni.

19

This 1,700-year-old painting of an Egyptian goose was found in one of the pyramids.

Not All Birds Can Fly

The ostrich can't fly, but it sure can run. When an enemy is nearby, an ostrich can run up to 60 miles per hour (96 km/hr). Penguins can't fly either, but they are excellent swimmers. They use their short wings in the same way a fish uses its flippers.

pelicans, which they kept for eggs. Although ostriches have been kept and bred for hundreds of years, they continue to be extremely aggressive.

The birds that have been most successfully domesticated—the goose, the pigeon, and the chicken—have certain traits in common.

- They live in flocks made up of family organizations and "pecking orders" that determine which animals are dominant. This type of social grouping makes animals easier to domesticate. For example, wolves, which evolved into dogs, normally live in packs.

- They are not skilled fliers. Because birds such as chickens and turkeys do not fly well, it was easier for ancient people to capture and keep them.

- They eat seeds. It is more difficult to domesticate birds that eat nectar or insects because finding and keeping food for them involves a great deal of time and effort.

Parrots, parakeets, and canaries were successfully domesticated because in the wild, they live in flocks and eat seeds. Parrots and parakeets are often very affectionate. Many enjoy interacting with people—sitting on their shoulders and nuzzling them. Because these birds have the ability to mimic speech or sing beautifully, people were

These hyacinth macaws are a type of parrot. They can be tamed because they live in flocks, eat seeds, and are very affectionate.

21

Pigeons being released from their cages

willing to invest the time and effort required to build cages to hold them. People also learned that it was very difficult for these birds to fly if just a few of their flight feathers were clipped.

It is more difficult to explain how pigeons and falcons were domesticated. Pigeons do not live in family groups and they are skilled fliers. However, it has been possible to train them to carry messages for us because they form a strong bond to a specific site. No matter where they are released, they will always return to the place they consider their home.

Falcons are solitary hunters, eat meat, and are excellent fliers. Because falcons can be exceptional sporting animals, modern falconers are willing to spend many hours training their birds.

2

GEESE: THE FIRST DOMESTICATED BIRDS

The Graylag goose was probably the first domesticated bird. It was tamed by people living in southeastern Europe about 20,000 years ago. It is easy to see why people formed an early relationship with the goose. It is a very social animal that has a family life similar to that of humans. Geese mate for life and show an intense devotion to their young. Baby geese—called goslings—display equally strong affection for their parents. When a pair of geese has

A graylag
goose

High Flyers

Birds can fly at very high altitudes, higher than the tallest mountains. Geese have been photographed flying at more than 5.5 miles (8.9 km) above the earth.

new goslings, their young from previous seasons often return to help raise the newborns.

Graylag geese may have been kept as "watchdogs," a role they still play in many farmyards. All geese are easily disturbed by unfamiliar sounds and will become noisy when a visitor or intruder approaches. Geese can also be extremely aggressive.

ARE YOU MY MOTHER?

Graylag geese that hatch and are raised under human care will treat their human foster parent just like a mother goose. Konrad Lorenz, a scientist who studied animal

MIGRATION

Millions of birds migrate each spring and fall, leaving their frozen homelands in the Northern Hemisphere to winter in the sunny south. Many birds fly halfway around the world.

Scientists believe that changes in day length tell birds when it's time to migrate. When the days get shorter in the fall, they know it's time to head south. Most migrating birds, especially the smaller ones, like to fly at night, when it is dark.

Birds follow fixed routes, or "flyways." These are the very same routes that their parents and ancestors used. North America has four main flyways: the Atlantic, the Mississippi, the Central, and the Pacific. Unless the birds are delayed by storms, they often arrive at their southern destination within a day or two of the same date each year.

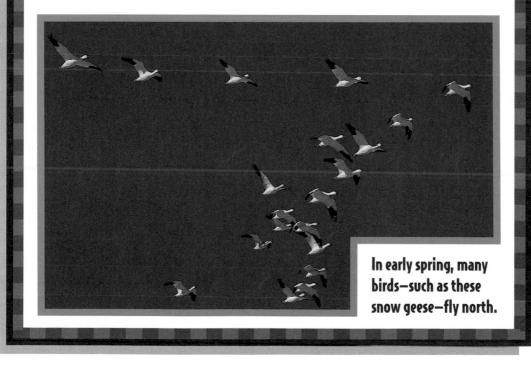

In early spring, many birds—such as these snow geese—fly north.

Konrad Lorenz with three of his geese

behavior, called this type of learning **imprinting**. For the most part, imprinting works only if a newborn gosling sees a human as soon as it hatches. In some cases, the gosling will treat a human as its mother if the person honks like a female goose.

Once a gosling imprints on someone, it follows that person everywhere and depends on the person for food and affection. When Lorenz imprinted several goslings on himself, they followed him wherever he went and even swam with him. As those geese grew, they continued to be friendly toward Lorenz. In a way, imprinting is like taming—it paves the way for domestication.

3 FROM RED JUNGLE FOWL TO CHICKEN

Over the last several thousand years, people have developed more than 200 **breeds** of chickens. Some lay brown eggs, while others lay white eggs. Some have excellent breast meat, but the meat on their thighs and legs is less tasty. Other chickens have fairly good meat on the thighs, legs, and breast.

The chicken's wild ancestor, the red jungle fowl, lives in the warm rain forests of southern Asia. **Archaeologists** have found 8,000-year-old chicken bones in parts of northeastern China. As a result, they believe

Red jungle fowl— the ancestor of the chicken— can still be found in some parts of Asia.

Breathing in the Shell

A bird's egg has many tiny air-holes—usually at the larger end, which is closest to the head of the unborn chick. The chick's lungs begin to work just before it breaks out of its shell.

that people must have bred chickens that could survive in the colder climate.

Ancient groups of people living in what is now India also domesticated chickens—but not for food. Instead, they kept the females for eggs and the males for entertainment. They would choose two roosters and force them to fight to the death. These "cockfights" are represented on 4,000-year-old coins. (Although cockfighting is illegal in the United States, roosters are still bred and raised for cockfighting in many other countries.)

Because chickens lay an egg every day, ancient Egyptian hieroglyphics used a chicken-shaped symbol to repre-

This painting, which appears on an ancient Greek vase, shows a cockfight.

Little Eggs, Big Eggs

The doctor bird, a kind of hummingbird that lives in Jamaica, lays the smallest bird eggs. One of these eggs is barely 1/2 inch (1.3 cm) in length and looks like a large pearl. Ostriches lay the largest bird eggs. Each one weighs about 3 pounds (1.4 kg).

sent fertility. The Egyptians were also the first group of people to develop a method for artificially incubating chicken eggs.

When Spanish explorers landed in the New World, they noticed that the native people of the Americas were raising chickens too. Because chickens originally came from Asia, archeologists and historians believe that Polynesians must have traveled to the Americas before Europeans did. Apparently, the Asian explorers carried chickens as food on long journeys.

29

A Victoria crowned pigeon (left), frillback pigeon (center) and nicobar pigeon (bottom) look very different from one another.

CHAPTER 5
FALCONRY AS A SPORT

Falconry involves training predatory birds, such as the peregrine falcon, to kill other birds and small animals. The peregrine falcon is a powerful flying machine with a bullet-shaped head, a streamlined body, and pointed wings that allow it to reach a diving speed of 175 miles per hour (282 km/hr).

Falconry may also include working with hawks, eagles, and other **raptors**. No matter which type of bird is used, falconry is extremely challenging because it is very difficult to tame these birds without damaging their keen hunting abilities.

Peregrine falcons are skilled hunters.

EAGLE EYES

Birds have better vision than any other kind of animal.

- A vulture can soar more than 1 mile (1.6 km) above the earth scanning the ground for **carrion**.
- A red-tailed hawk drifting on warm currents of air can spot a little meadow mouse creeping through the grass 100 feet (30 m) below.
- A sparrow hawk's eyesight is eight times more powerful than a human's.

Birds have very large eyes relative to their body size. In fact, in most birds, the eyes are actually larger than the brain. Birds also have many more cells on their **retina**—the part of the eye that receives the visual image—than other animals.

Although a bird cannot move its eyes as a human can, it can turn its head to see in every direction. Some birds can even swivel their neck to look directly behind them. And because a bird's eyes are on the sides of its head, it can look in two places at once.

A red-tailed hawk in flight

Falcons and other raptors are not bred. They must be captured when they are very young and patiently trained. In the training process, which was perfected more than 500 years ago, food is used as a reward to control the bird's behavior. Falconers usually train their birds to attack pigeons, partridge, grouse, crows, and rabbits.

First, the bird must learn to sit on its owner's arm. The owner wears a glove made of thick cloth or leather for

Falconers wear heavy gloves to protect their arms and hands from their birds' sharp claws.

protection from the bird's sharp claws. Initially, the bird is anchored to the glove with a line attached to its leg.

The falconer then takes the bird to a large open area. At this point, the bird wears a hood so that it doesn't become distracted and fly off too soon. When the falconer or a hunting dog spots prey, the falcon is unhooded and set free. (Some people believe that coordinating the movements and behaviors of two domesticated animals raises animal training to the level of an art.)

Using its powerful wings, the bird flies above the prey, then dives down at lightning speed and strikes the victim with enormous force. In most cases, the target is killed instantly. Unlike a wild raptor, which would then eat the prey, the trained falcon returns to its owner's arm. The falconer feeds the bird to reward it. Then, the falconer, or an assistant, fetches the kill.

THE HISTORY OF FALCONRY

Falconry was developed more than 4,000 years ago in eastern and central Asia. Birds were used because they could strike down animals beyond the range of the hunter's primitive weapons. Gradually, however, falconry developed into a respected pastime for wealthy and powerful people.

When the famous European explorer Marco Polo returned from his journey to China, he reported that the Great Kahn had 10,000 falconers and often went on hunting expeditions to the eastern part of his kingdom. The Khan traveled in a carriage supported by four elephants and was accompanied by twelve falconers. Other men went on the trip to spot prey. When these men noticed a bird overhead, they gave a signal. The curtains of the Khan's

This painting from a book by Marco Polo shows the Great Kahn hunting with a falcon.

carriage were opened and one of the falcons was released. The ruler watched as the hunting bird attacked its victim.

Eventually, falconry spread to Europe. Knights returning from Holy Wars in the Middle East brought back Arab falconers and their hawks. These knights often valued their birds as much as their swords or their horses. Soon, the rulers of Asia began to exchange birds with the kings of Europe. Eventually, queens, czars, and even popes had birds.

Today, falconry is still popular in many parts of the world. In Europe, falconers often gather together at prestigious clubs, such as the Falconers Club in England, the Loo Club in Holland, and the Club de Champagne in France. The sport also continues in China, India, and the Middle East.

6

CAGED BIRDS AS PETS

Polly want a cracker?

While most of the birds that have been domesticated are used for food or sport, caged birds are kept simply for their beauty or their song. These birds were first tamed by the ancient Chinese. Since then, caged birds—especially canaries and parakeets—have been extensively bred to create different varieties, with interesting colors, plumage, and songs.

This Chinese man enjoys the beautiful song of his pet bird.

A LOOK AT PARROTS

More than 300 different species of birds can be called parrots. Relatives of the parrots include parakeets, budgerigars, lories, lorikeets, macaws, cockatoos, cockatiels, keas, rosellas, and lovebirds. Their bright colors and their ability to mimic speech make parrots very popular pets. Not all parrots are brightly colored, though. Some have colors that blend with their surroundings, and a few kinds are

Feathered Monkeys

Parrots are great imitators. Not only can they mimic our speech, but they whistle tunes. They also like to imitate movements. Cockatoos are so comical that they are sometimes called "feathered monkeys." They do gymnastics, dance, rock back and forth, and perform outlandish tricks.

These colorful cockatoos are one type of parrot.

Counting Birds

Are parakeets intelligent? Their playfulness and ability to learn tricks certainly suggests that they are intelligent. In one scientific experiment, birds were taught to count. Each bird demonstrated its ability by picking up the number of seeds indicated. The parakeet understood the meaning of the numbers 1 through 6. In the same experiment, doves learned to count to 5 and ravens learned to count to 7.

By the 1880s, a farm in Toulouse, France, had 20,000 breeding birds. Today, there are probably more parakeets in captivity than there are in the wild.

Unfortunately, the practice of capturing parrots and selling them as pets has brought many species to the verge of extinction. As a result, many parrots—especially those in the Amazon region of South America—have been placed on the international Red List of Threatened Animals.

PARAKEETS MAKE GREAT PETS

Like many other domesticated birds, parakeets live in flocks in the wild. As a result, if a human raises them, they will show great affection and devotion toward that person. In fact, when a parakeet is let out of its cage, it spends most of its time perching on the head, shoulder, or hand of its human guardian.

In the wild, parakeets often groom each others' feathers. Tame birds show the same behavior when they try to groom the skin and hair of their owner. Some even try to feed their human guardian by regurgitating shelled seeds near that person's mouth.

Parakeets have a wonderful ability to mimic human speech. Children and women are said to make the best teachers because their voices are clearer and higher in pitch. A parakeet that is 5 to 6 weeks old and has no contact with other birds will quickly learn to say words. This quality, along with its general playfulness, makes the parakeet one of the most endearing pets. Even though a parakeet doesn't understand our speech, its ability to say words is entertaining and creates a feeling of closeness between the bird and its owner.

Talking Sense?

Do talking birds know what they're saying? No, but they seem to when they learn to say phrases in the right situations. A parrot, for example, may learn to say "Good morning," in the morning, or "Good night," at night. The parrot does not know the meaning of "morning" or "night." It is simply mimicking the situation in which a person says these phrases.

Parakeets make great pets.

49